ELLIOTT'S GUIDE TO DINOSAURS

ELLIOTT'S GUIDE TO DINOSAURS

ELLIOTT SEAH

GREYSTONE BOOKS

Vancouver/Berkeley

Copyright © 2016 by Greystone Books
Originally published in French by Éditions Multimondes as *Petit Guide des Dinosaures* in 2015

16 17 18 19 20   6 5 4 3 2

Greystone Books Ltd.
www.greystonebooks.com

Cataloguing data available from Library and Archives Canada
ISBN 978-1-77164-237-8 (cloth)
ISBN 978-1-77164-238-5 (epub)

Editing for English-language edition by Catherine Marjoribanks
Editing for French-language edition by Christine Cade, Lise Morin, Jean-Marc Gagnon, Sarah Jalbert
Jacket and interior design by Christine Cade and Nayeli Jimenez
Cover illustration by Elliott Seah
Illustrations on page 22, 28, and 34 by Elliott Seah
Printed and bound in China by 1010 Printing International Ltd.

We gratefully acknowledge the support of the Canada Council for the Arts, the British Columbia Arts Council, the Province of British Columbia through the Book Publishing Tax Credit, and the Government of Canada through the Canada Book Fund for our publishing activities.

Canadä

Greystone Books is committed to reducing the consumption of old-growth forests in the books it publishes.

CONTENTS

Hi, I'm Seahsaurus!
I'll tag along as you read to explain different
things throughout the book.

To everyone who helped me with this
book and to everyone who will read it.

FASTEN YOUR SEATBELTS!

This guide to dinosaurs includes a lot of information for both beginners and the more advanced. You'll discover many species of dinosaurs, their predecessors, and their descendants.

I can't believe that I wrote this book when I was just eight years old. Fasten your seatbelts and off we go!

Elliott Seah

Elliott Seah
Author/Illustrator
www.paleodinos.jimdo.com

A MESSAGE FROM ELLIOTT'S PARENTS

This book originated as part of the Marguerite-Bourgeoys School Board's program for Gifted and Talented Students. After taking a series of classes in paleontology, Elliott, who was eight years old, decided to write a guide to share his newfound knowledge and his passion for dinosaurs. While working on this project he had the opportunity to collaborate with Christine Cade, a graphic designer who shared her love of paleontology with Elliott. We're very proud of Elliott's work, but even more proud of the motivation and determination that he showed throughout this adventure.

A MESSAGE FROM CHRISTINE CADE

Paleontology has always fascinated me. Although I ended up choosing another career, I never lost my passion for the subject. In 2014, I wanted to share my knowledge of paleontology and, as luck would have it, Elliott and I were introduced.

Over the course of many months, I came to know Elliott as a boy with a lively mind and infinite curiosity. Through hard work and dedication, he came to be remarkably knowledgeable about the subject. Elliott, hang on to those strengths! Who knows? Maybe they will lead you to discover the Seahsaurus!

Elliott Seah, with Hans Larsson, paleontologist, and Christine Cade

DID YOU KNOW . . .

- paleontologists Jack Horner and Hans Larsson are trying to bring dinosaurs back to life by genetically modifying chickens to recreate a dinosaur species? They have nicknamed this new creature *Chickenosaurus*.

- some herbivores would swallow pebbles to help them digest plants? Paleontologists call these pebbles "gastroliths."

- dinosaur bones have gone into outer space?

- the most complete *Tyrannosaurus rex* skeleton contains 80% of its original bone structure and is displayed at the Field Museum in Chicago?

- the country with the greatest variety of dinosaur species is the United States, followed by Canada, China, Argentina, Mongolia, and England?

- *Spinosaurus* was a semi-aquatic dinosaur?

(Above) Canadian flag, NASA space shuttle, American flag
(Below) Field Museum of Chicago, Jack Horner

NEW DISCOVERIES

Even though dinosaur species were identified for the first time about two hundred years ago, we're still discovering new species today. Here are a few recent finds:

- *Nanuqsaurus*, a smaller cousin of *Tyrannosaurus*, was discovered in the Arctic. Nanuq is the word for polar bear in Inuktitut.

- A giant sauropod, *Dreadnoughtus*, was discovered in the south of Argentina. Its name comes from the word "dreadnought," which describes a huge battleship.

- A predator by the name of *Qianzhousaurus sinensis* was discovered in the south of China. It was nicknamed "Pinocchio rex" because of its long snout.

(Top left) Nanuqsaurus *skull*
(Top right) Illustration of *Nanuqsaurus*

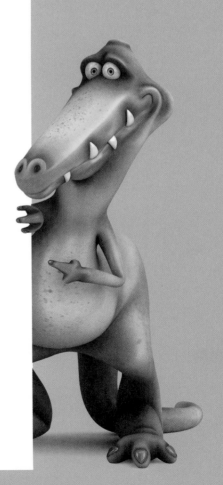

BEFORE DINOSAURS...

When the Earth was formed 4.5 billion years ago, there was no life at all on our planet. The first life forms appeared 3.8 billion years ago, but they were just simple single-celled organisms. Since then, new species have appeared and become extinct through evolution. Evolution is the process by which species change across many generations.

The first fish appeared in the period called the Cambrian, 530 million years ago. The first plants on land date back to the period called the Ordovician, 450 million years ago. Then came the first amphibians, during the Devonian period, about 400 million years ago, and later the first reptiles, during the Carboniferous period, about 310 million years ago.

During the Permian period, large mammal ancestors like Dimetrodon wandered the Earth. They looked a lot like dinosaurs, but they weren't actually dinosaurs. They were synapsids—that means they had one opening in their skulls behind each eye socket. Dinosaurs were diapsids—that means that they had two openings in their skulls behind each eye socket. Mammals, including humans like us, are all synapsids. Living examples of diapsids include crocodiles, lizards, snakes, and birds.

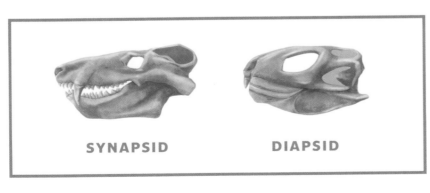

SYNAPSID   DIAPSID

DIMETRODON

Species include:

Dimetrodon grandis
Dimetrodon limatus
Dimetrodon teutonis
Dimetrodon borealis

· ·

 United States, Germany, Canada

BEGINNING OF THE PERMIAN
295 to 262 million years ago

SYNAPSID

APPEARANCE: 1.7 to 4.6 meters in length, 28 to 250 kilograms

DIET: Carnivorous

LOCOMOTION: Quadruped, crawling posture

MUSEUM WITH SKELETONS: National Museum of Natural History, Washington, DC (*Dimetrodon grandis*)

DISTINGUISHING FEATURE
· · · · · · · · ·
A dorsal sail allowed it to regulate its body temperature.

THE ORIGINS
OF DINOSAURS

Dinosaurs were the giant reptile descendants of the archosaurs, a group of species that also includes crocodiles and birds.

THE GEOLOGIC TIME SCALE

This is a timeline that represents the history of the planet Earth. It is divided into four eras. Each era is divided into periods, which are then divided into epochs. (MYA stands for Million Years Ago.)

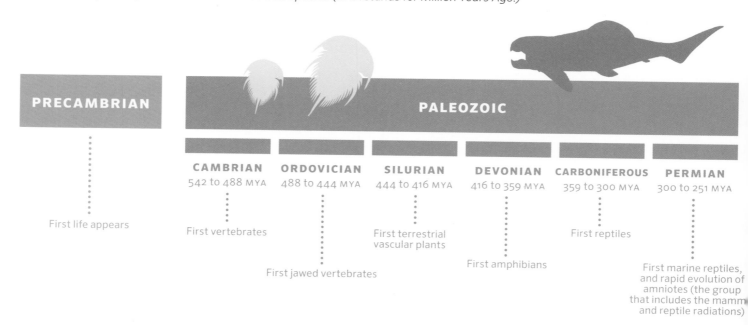

PRECAMBRIAN

PALEOZOIC

CAMBRIAN	**ORDOVICIAN**	**SILURIAN**	**DEVONIAN**	**CARBONIFEROUS**	**PERMIAN**
542 to 488 MYA	488 to 444 MYA	444 to 416 MYA	416 to 359 MYA	359 to 300 MYA	300 to 251 MYA

First life appears

First vertebrates

First jawed vertebrates

First terrestrial
vascular plants

First amphibians

First reptiles

First marine reptiles,
and rapid evolution of
amniotes (the group
that includes the mamm
and reptile radiations)

At the end of the Permian period, 251 million years ago, a mass extinction took place, which means that a huge number of Earth's species died off. More than 90% of life forms died then. Those that survived quickly re-explored a new Earth and evolved into many of the main lineages of animals and plants we have today.

With reduced competition for resources on Earth, dinosaurs were able to become the dominant land animal for the next 150 million years.

Dinosaurs first appeared at the end of the Triassic period during the Mesozoic era.

Before the dinosaurs, there had already been three other big extinctions that led to the disappearance of many species living on Earth.

During the late Palaeozoic and early Mesozoic periods, Earth's land mass was one giant "supercontinent," which we call Pangaea. Later, this land mass divided and the new continents drifted apart.

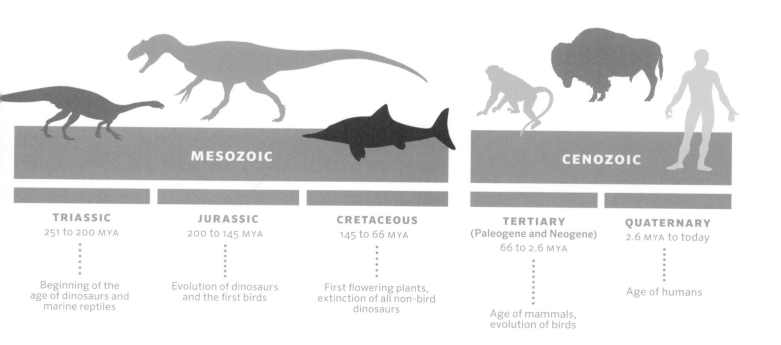

MESOZOIC

CENOZOIC

TRIASSIC
251 to 200 MYA

JURASSIC
200 to 145 MYA

CRETACEOUS
145 to 66 MYA

TERTIARY
(Paleogene and Neogene)
66 to 2.6 MYA

QUATERNARY
2.6 MYA to today

Beginning of the age of dinosaurs and marine reptiles

Evolution of dinosaurs and the first birds

First flowering plants, extinction of all non-bird dinosaurs

Age of mammals, evolution of birds

Age of humans

DINOSAUR DIETS

We can often tell what a dinosaur ate by looking at the shape of its teeth.

Herbivore: plant-eating

Carnivore: meat-eating (other dinosaurs, lizards, etc.)

Omnivore: ate a variety of food including roots, plants, meat, insects, and fis

Piscivore: primarily fish-eating

Insectivore: insect-eating

②

①

③

④

1. The tooth of *Spinosaurus*, a piscivore. Its conical, pointy shape helped to pierce and hold on to slippery fish.
2. The pointy and serrated knife-like tooth of *Allosaurus*, a carnivore. Carnivores had pointy teeth for grabbing prey, and serrated teeth for cutting meat.
3. Teeth of *Diplodocus*, a herbivore. Their flat shape made it easier to tear off leaves or other plants before swallowing.
4. Dental battery (group of teeth) of a hadrosaur, a family of duck-billed herbivorous dinosaurs. A dental battery was made up of hundreds of small teeth that covered the large surface area of a hadrosaur's jaw. The teeth would constantly be replaced by new teeth when they wore down. This particular tooth configuration made it easy to grind up large quantities of food.

THE DIFFERENCE BETWEEN SAURISCHIANS AND ORNITHISCHIANS

Dinosaurs can be divided into two big orders, or groups, depending on their anatomy:

- **saurischians:** dinosaurs with a lizard-like pelvis

- **ornithischians:** dinosaurs with a bird-like pelvis

The structure of the pelvic bones determines whether a dinosaur belongs to one order or the other.

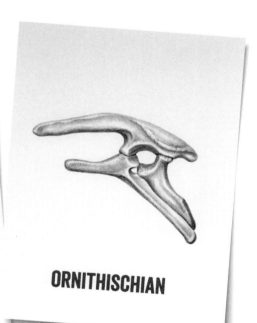

ORNITHISCHIAN

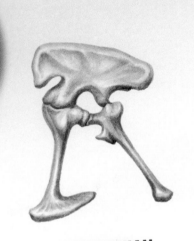

SAURISCHIAN

The **saurischian** order includes the large dinosaurs known as the sauropods (like *Diplodocus*) and the theropods. All carnivorous dinosaurs (like *Tyrannosaurus rex*) and the first birds (like *Archaeopteryx*) are theropods.

The **ornithischian** order includes the frilled ceratopsians (such as *Triceratops*), the duck-billed hadrosaurs (such as *Parasaurolophus*), the bone-headed pachycephalosaurs (such as *Pachycephalosaurus*), and the armored dinosaurs (like *Stegosaurus* and *Ankylosaurus*).

ATTACK

Dinosaurs used different means of attack. For example, some herbivores, like *Pachycephalosaurus*, had bony skulls, which they used to butt heads in order to establish themselves as the dominant male in a group, or to impress a female. They may have also used their heads to crash into predators. Carnivores used their sharp teeth to wound, cut, or eat their prey. Carnivores could also use their excellent eyesight, their speed, and their sense of smell to hunt.

DEFENSE

Dinosaurs had different ways of defending themselves against predators. Some herbivores used their tails like whips (*Diplodocus*) or clubs (*Ankylosaurus*) to hit their enemies.

Ankylosaurus' body was covered by an armor made of bony plates from head to tail—and even around its eyes and nose! Also, a theory suggests that some hadrosaurs used the long tubular crests on their heads like an instrument, to make loud noises to call each other or to scare their predators.

EVEN TYRANNOSAURUS COULDN'T PIERCE THIS ARMOR!

REPRODUCTION

Dinosaurs were oviparous, which means they laid eggs. Their eggs came in different shapes and sizes, depending on the species. A female dinosaur could lay one or many eggs, which were placed in a nest on the ground.

Some scientists believe that female sauropods had a tube that would deposit the eggs on the ground while they walked in a straight line, which would have prevented the eggs from falling from a height of at least 2 meters and breaking!

After the eggs were laid, depending on the species, one of three things might have happened:

❶ in the case of some carnivores, the female would chase the male away before incubating the eggs

❷ in the case of most carnivores and herbivores, the female would incubate the eggs while the male brought her food

❸ in the case of most sauropods, the eggs would be abandoned, and the babies would have to learn how to survive on their own

The name *Maiasaura* means "good mother" because these dinosaur females raised their young.

Carnivorous dinosaurs taught their young how to hunt and how to defend themselves by the time they were two years old. Dinosaurs knew nearly everything they needed to know by the age of five and could leave their parents. In comparison, humans continue to learn throughout their lives.

SOCIAL LIFE

Dinosaurs were social beings. They could live, hunt, and migrate in groups. There was safety in numbers so they often stuck together for greater security, to take care of their young, or to hunt effectively. We know from skeleton deposits that dinosaurs generally lived in groups and sometimes died together.

WHAT COLORS WERE THE DINOSAURS?

Dinosaurs are drawn with all sorts of different colors, but the artists are mostly guessing. Nobody knows what colors they actually were, except in the case of species for which we have found fossilized feathers containing coloration. In the case of *Anchiornis*, for example, scientists were able to determine that its feathers were the colors in the picture you see here. But since an ability to see color is often associated with a colorful appearance, and we know that most reptiles can see color, we can imagine that at least some of the dinosaurs were pretty colorful creatures.

GETTING AROUND

Some dinosaurs were quadrupeds, which means they walked on four legs like the dinosaur below, while others were bipeds and walked on two legs like *Coelophysis* (page 24).

Dinosaurs could be graviportal (their bodies built to support their heavy weight) or cursorial (their bodies built to run very fast). Their ability to run quickly depended on their weight and their anatomic structure, including the shape of their legs and the number of toes they had.

DINOSAUR SKELETONS AND HUMAN SKELETONS

Dinosaurs were a very diverse group of animals, but if we look at their skeletons and compare them to those of humans, there are a lot of bones that are common to both. The following bones can be found in both dinosaurs and humans: the skull (cranium), the spine (vertebrae), the ribs, the shoulder blade (scapula), the collar bone (clavicle), the upper arm (humerus), the two forearm bones (radius and ulna), the wrist (carpals), the long bones in the hand (metacarpals), the fingers and toes (phalanges), the pelvic bones (ilium, ischium, and pubis), the upper leg (femur), the lower leg (tibia and fibula), the ankle bones (tarsals), and the long bones in the foot (metatarsals).

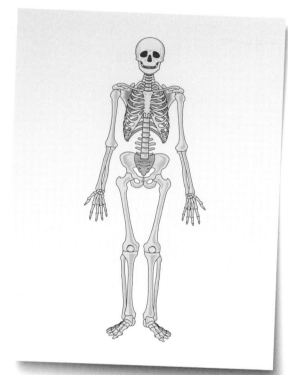

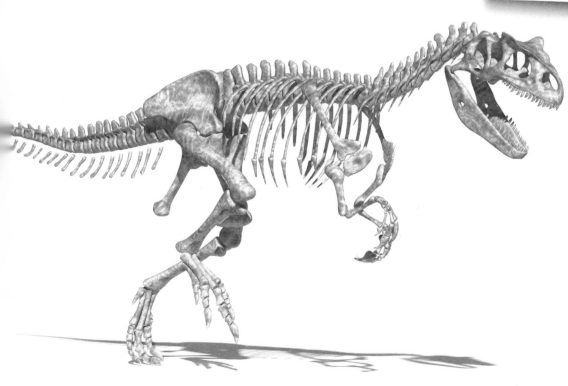

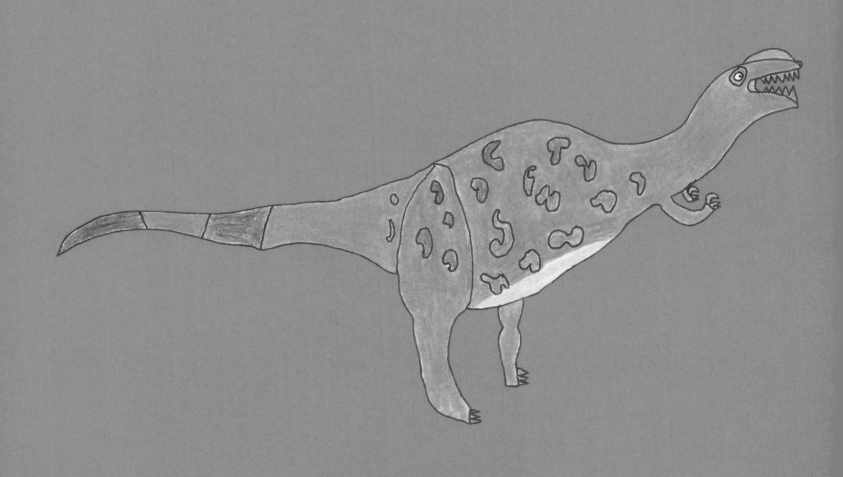

DINOSAURS OF THE TRIASSIC

251 TO 200 MILLION YEARS AGO

· ·

The first dinosaurs lived during the Triassic period, which began 251 million years ago and ended 200 million years ago, when the Jurassic period began. According to paleontologists, dinosaurs appeared only towards the end of the Triassic period. Even though there wasn't as much variety in the dinosaurs of the Triassic as there was in the Jurassic and Cretaceous periods, several differences between the species led to a classification according to different criteria such as size, anatomy, locomotion, and diet.

(Opposite) Drawing of Coelophysis

COELOPHYSIS

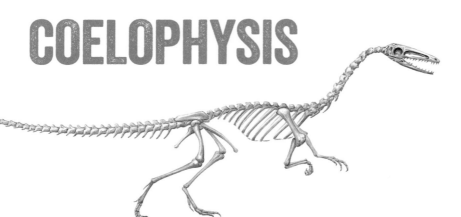

Coelophysis bauri

· ·

 New Mexico (United States)

TRIASSIC
203 to 196 million years ago

GROUP: Saurischian

APPEARANCE: 3 meters long, 25 kilograms

DIET: Carnivore (it ate small animals)

LOCOMOTION: Biped, cursorial

MUSEUM WITH SKELETON:
Cleveland Museum of Natural History,
Cleveland, Ohio

DISTINGUISHING FEATURES

· ·

A site containing many *Coelophysis* skeletons leads us to believe that they lived in groups. *Coelophysis* was also the second dinosaur to go into space, after *Maiasaura*. Astronauts in the *Endeavor* space shuttle took a *Coelophysis* skull to the Mir space station during a 1998 mission.

PLATEOSAURUS

Plateosaurus engenhardti

· ·

 Southern Germany

UPPER TRIASSIC
214 to 204 million years ago

GROUP: Saurischian

APPEARANCE: 8.5 meters long, 1.9 tonnes

DIET: Herbivore

LOCOMOTION: Biped and quadruped (could do both)

MUSEUM WITH SKELETON:
Geosciences Department at Eberhard Karls University of Tübingen, Germany

LESSEMSAURUS

Lessemsaurus sauropoides

 Argentina

TRIASSIC
210 million years ago

GROUP: Saurischian

APPEARANCE: 10 meters long, 2 tonnes

DIET: Herbivore

LOCOMOTION: Quadruped, graviportal

MUSEUM WITH SKELETON:
Bernardino Rivadavia Natural Sciences Museum,
Buenos Aires, Argentina

DISTINGUISHING FEATURES

Even though it's the size of a prosauropod, the *Lessemsaurus* had bones like those of a sauropod, which is why it is classified as one of the first sauropods. It fed on cycads, a plant that did not contain a lot of nutrients, so to make up for it, it had to eat a lot, and often.

HERRERASAURUS

Herrerasaurus ischigualastensis

 Argentina

TRIASSIC
225 million years ago

GROUP: Saurischian

APPEARANCE: 3 meters long, 100 kilograms

DIET: Carnivore

LOCOMOTION: Biped, cursorial

MUSEUM WITH SKELETON:
Senckenberg Natural History Museum,
Frankfurt, Germany

DISTINGUISHING FEATURES

Even though *Herrerasaurus* was only 3 meters long, it was the largest carnivorous dinosaur of its time! Its arms were short but it had long claws for grabbing prey. Its name comes from Don Victorino Herrera, a rancher who discovered three incomplete skeletons of this dinosaur in rocky ground in Argentina.

DINOSAURS OF THE JURASSIC

200 TO 145 MILLION YEARS AGO

After the great extinction of the Triassic period, dinosaurs evolved again and new, giant species (sauropods) appeared.

Earth's continents didn't always look like the continents of today, because they are always moving. They move extremely slowly, about 3 centimeters per year (slower than your fingernails grow). At one point, Pangaea, which was one big "supercontinent," separated and became two large continents: a southern land mass called Gondwana, and a northern land mass called Laurasia. This split allowed dinosaurs on each land mass to evolve separately for millions of years, and explains why many of today's continents have different kinds of dinosaur fossils. Birds, having evolved from certain theropod dinosaurs, also appeared at the end of the Jurassic period.

(Opposite) Drawing of Dacentrurus

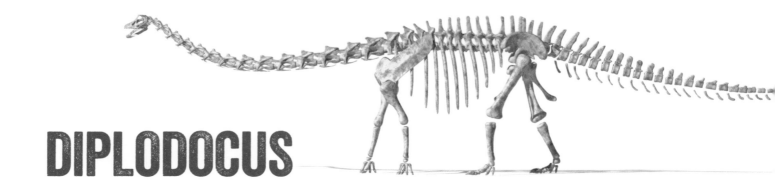

DIPLODOCUS

Diplodocus longus
(one of many species in this family)

- -

 Colorado, Utah (United States)

JURASSIC
154 to 150 million years ago

GROUP: Saurischian

APPEARANCE: 25 meters long, 12 tonnes

DIET: Herbivore (ate leaves from treetops)

LOCOMOTION: Quadruped, graviportal

MUSEUM WITH SKELETON:
Carnegie Museum of Natural History,
Pittsburgh, Pennsylvania

DISTINGUISHING FEATURES

- - - - - - - - - - - -

Diplodocus attacked and defended itself by using its tail to strike its enemies. Its tail, which served as a powerful whip, was about half the total length of its body.

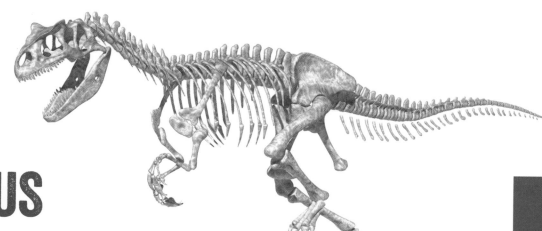

ALLOSAURUS

Allosaurus fragilis
(the most well-known species)

 Colorado and Utah (United States), Portugal, Tanzania

JURASSIC
155 to 150 million years ago

GROUP: Saurischian

APPEARANCE: 12 meters long, 1 to 4 tonnes

DIET: Carnivore (ate large herbivorous dinosaurs)

LOCOMOTION: Biped, cursorial

MUSEUM WITH SKELETON:
San Diego Natural History Museum, San Diego, California

DISTINGUISHING FEATURES

This "different lizard" was at the top of the food chain during the Jurassic period, which means that it didn't have any predators and it preyed on other dinosaurs, including other carnivores.

"Allo" means **different** in Greek. *"Saurus"* means **lizard.**

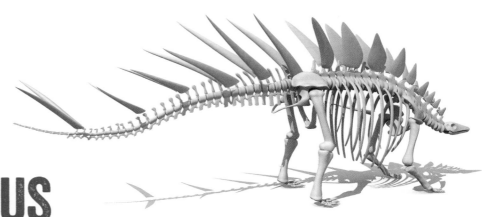

DACENTRURUS

Dacentrurus armatus

· · · · · · · · · · · · · · · · · · ·

 Western Europe

JURASSIC
163 to 150 million years ago

GROUP: Ornithischian

APPEARANCE: 7.5 meters long, 5 tonnes

DIET: Herbivore

LOCOMOTION: Quadruped, graviportal

MUSEUM WITH SKELETON:
Natural History Museum,
London, England

This dinosaur had three kinds of spikes
of different shapes and sizes on its
shoulders, back, and tail. It looked kind
of like a porcupine. It used the spikes
on its tail and shoulders to attack and
defend. The spikes on its back con-
tained many blood vessels, which could
be used for display (like blushing) or to
regulate body temperature.

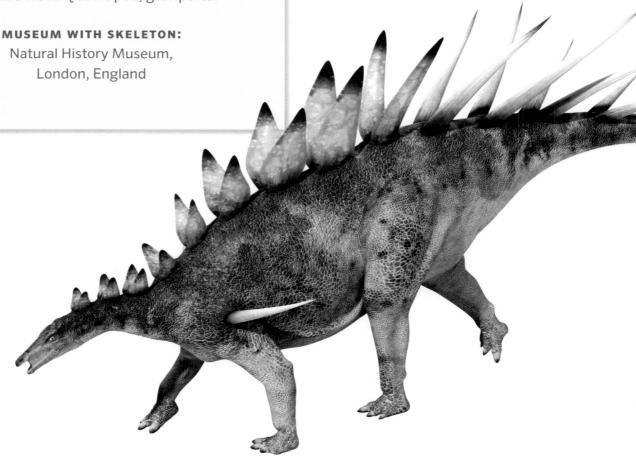

ARCHAEOPTERYX

Archaeopteryx lithographica

· ·

 Germany

JURASSIC
150 million years ago

GROUP: Saurischian

APPEARANCE: 0.5 meters long, 0.5 kilograms

DIET: Insectivore

LOCOMOTION: Biped, cursorial

MUSEUM WITH SKELETON:
Museum of Natural History,
Berlin, Germany

DISTINGUISHING FEATURES

· · · · · · · · · · · · · · · · · ·

Archaeopteryx was the first bird, but it couldn't fly the way birds do now. Instead, it stayed close to the ground but used its wings to lift and glide short distances. Today's birds don't have teeth, but *Archaeopteryx*, a theropod, had a mouthful! It also had three claws on each wing and its bones were hollow.

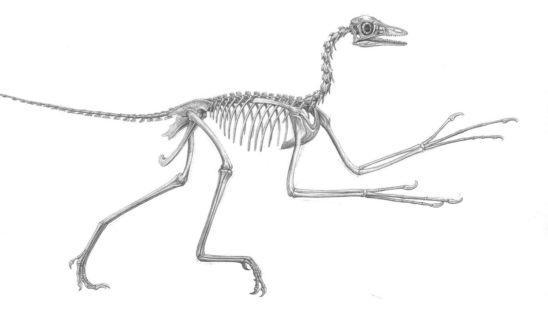

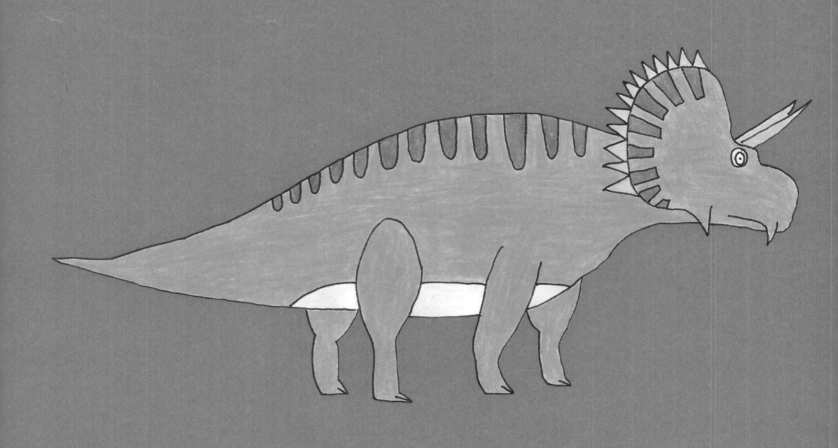

DINOSAURS OF THE CRETACEOUS

145 TO 66 MILLION YEARS AGO

The Cretaceous is the period from 145 to 66 million years ago. It was the time of giants, when the largest species of dinosaurs lived. There was greater variety in the types of dinosaurs alive during the Cretaceous than in any earlier period.

(Opposite) Drawing of Triceratops

TRICERATOPS

Triceratops horridus

· ·

 Canada and the United States

LATE CRETACEOUS
68 to 66 million years ago

GROUP: Ornithischian

APPEARANCE: 9 meters long, 6 to 12 tonnes

DIET: Herbivore

LOCOMOTION: Quadruped, graviportal

MUSEUM WITH SKELETON:
Royal Tyrrell Museum,
Drumheller, Alberta

DISTINGUISHING FEATURES

· ·

Triceratops is one of the group of ceratopsians that all have a bony frill at the back of the skull, often in the shape of a fan. *Triceratops* and *Torosaurus*, which were thought to be two separate species, each had three horns on their head. Now they're considered to be part of the same species, with the larger *Torosaurus* identified as an adult *Triceratops*. Because *Triceratops* was named first, we've kept the name *Triceratops*.

TYRANNOSAURUS

• • • • • • • • • • • • •

Tyrannosaurus rex had the most powerful bite of any land animal in history—anywhere from 12,800 to 40,000 pounds per square inch. In comparison, the human bite is about 120 pounds per square inch, and Nile crocodiles, the animal with the strongest bite alive today, have a biting power of up to 7,700 pounds per square inch. Also, some scientists believe that *Tyrannosaurus* might have had feathers!

Tyrannosaurus rex

• • • • • • • • • • • • • • • • •

Canada and the United States

LATE CRETACEOUS
67 to 65 million years ago

GROUP: Saurischian

APPEARANCE: 12 meters long, 6 tonnes

DIET: Carnivore

LOCOMOTION: Biped and cursorial

MUSEUM WITH SKELETON:
Jurassic Museum of Asturias, Spain

THERIZINOSAURUS

Therizinosaurus cheloniformis

· ·

 Mongolia, China,
and the United States

CRETACEOUS
70 million years ago

GROUP: Saurischian

APPEARANCE: 11 meters long, 5 tonnes

DIET: Omnivore or herbivore:
fossil evidence suggests that it had both
leaf-eating teeth and a front beak

MOVEMENT: Biped

MUSEUM WITH SKELETON:
Museum of Northern Arizona,
Flagstaff, Arizona

DISTINGUISHING FEATURES

· · · · · · · · · · · · · · ·

Therizinosaurus had claws that were
a meter long, arms that were 2.5
meters long, and a total height of 6
meters or more. With claws like that,
it could almost have scratched its
own back, but it probably used them
to uproot plants, just as the giant
ground sloth used to do.

TROODON

Troodon formosus

· · · · · · · · · · · · · · · · · · · ·

 United States and Canada

CRETACEOUS
76 million years ago

GROUP: Saurischian

APPEARANCE: 2 meters long, 50 kilograms

DIET: Carnivore

LOCOMOTION: Biped, cursorial

MUSEUM WITH SKELETON:
Perot Museum of Nature and Science,
Dallas, Texas

DISTINGUISHING FEATURES

· · · · · · · · · · · · · · · · · ·

Troodon was the most intelligent of the dinosaurs. It had a brain the size of a golf ball and was as smart as an ostrich—a real genius among dinosaurs. *Troodon* ate different kinds of small animals so its teeth had different shapes. Its prey probably included insects, small reptiles, and mammals. Its large eyes, which were pointed slightly forward, made it a good night hunter.

EXTINCTION OF
THE DINOSAURS

In total, five mass extinctions have marked the evolution of Earth. First, there was the **Ordovician-Silurian** extinction, in which 70% of all species disappeared. Next was a series of **Devonian** extinctions, in which 70% of all species died out. Then came the **Permian** extinction, in which more than 90% of all species died out, leading to the development of dinosaurs. After the **Triassic** extinction, in which 75% of all species went extinct, dinosaurs were left as the dominant land animals. The last was the **Cretaceous** extinction, in which 75% of all species, including all non-avian dinosaurs, became extinct. If you don't remember the order, see the Geologic Time Scale on page 14 and 15.

What caused the great extinction of the dinosaurs? In the past, many people believed that dinosaurs died because of the cold or other environmental reasons. But paleontologists now believe that the extinction, which happened 66 million years ago at the end of the **Cretaceous** period, was caused by an asteroid (a large rock from space) hitting the Earth at the Yucatan Peninsula in Mexico. The giant crater left by the asteroid indicates that the collision was extremely violent.

It is believed that the asteroid's impact caused the eruption of many volcanoes. The smoke from these volcanoes blocked the sun's light for many years, causing plants to die. Herbivores died not long after because they had nothing to eat. And without the large herbivores, the carnivores couldn't feed themselves, and they also died out as a result.

Many animals—like some mammals, avian dinosaurs, and reptiles—were able to survive perhaps because of their small size and their diverse diets, which allowed them to feed on whatever small amounts of food were available.

AFTER THE DINOSAURS

Birds are descendants of dinosaurs. Feathered dinosaurs of the "raptor" category were the direct ancestors of birds.

After the Cretaceous extinction, the surviving life quickly diversified and spread over Earth's land and seas. Mammals, like the mammoth (below), dominated Earth after the dinosaurs disappeared.

It's impossible to know how or why certain species survived extinctions. After all, there were no humans around to take notes or tell stories. But we can find out what survived and what didn't survive by studying the rocks around fossils.

Some mammals may have survived the extinction that killed the dinosaurs because of their smaller size and their ability to live in sheltered areas or underground. But humans didn't evolve immediately after the extinction at the end of the Cretaceous period; we came along many millions of years later, and we descended from primates. The first early humans lived about 7 million years ago. The first *Homo sapiens*, the species to which we belong, appeared only 1 million years ago. *Homo sapiens* is the only surviving species of human being.

The dinosaurs weren't the only ones to disappear from the planet. Marine reptiles and flying reptiles also became extinct. However, some avian dinosaurs survived and evolved into modern birds.

(Opposite) bald eagle, mammoth
(Above) marine reptile, flying reptile

A PALEONTOLOGIST'S TOOLS

Paleontologists use a number of tools in their work: the shovel, the chisel, the pick, the trowel, the paintbrush, and the soft brush. These tools are used to extract fossils from the rock and remove debris.

 The **shovel** is used to remove sand and rocks.

 The **chisel** is a sort of pick used to carve and crack rock.

 The **pick** and **hammer** help remove the rock around the fossil.

 Paleontologists use the **trowel** to remove dirt.

 A geological map, which indicates the type of rock in a given location, is also a useful tool. A **compass** helps paleontologists to orient themselves and find the dig site. And a GPS (Global Positioning System) provides even more precise navigation.

 Paleontologists also need two **brushes,** one big and one small, to remove dust from the fossil, **newspaper** and **plaster** to wrap the fossil, and a **camera** to record what they find.

FROM THE DIG TO THE LAB

The work of the paleontologist begins at the dig site and ends at the laboratory.

First, paleontologists set up camp on a site where fossils have been found. They'll need to live there, since the work can last many months and most fossils are found far from cities, towns, and hotels.

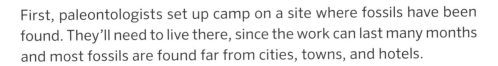

After they find a fossil, they must remove the rock that surrounds it. Then they have to draw a plan of the site, to help identify the bones and organize future digs.

They surround the fossils in plaster, because the fossils are ancient and can break easily. Then the paleontologists dig the fossils out of the earth. They sometimes need levers to help lift heavy fossils.

Finally, the fossils are transported to the laboratory by truck, train, boat, or plane. In the lab, the paleontologists do research on the bones, comparing them to existing or extinct species.

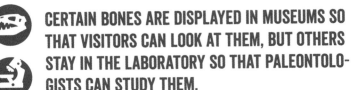

CERTAIN BONES ARE DISPLAYED IN MUSEUMS SO THAT VISITORS CAN LOOK AT THEM, BUT OTHERS STAY IN THE LABORATORY SO THAT PALEONTOLOGISTS CAN STUDY THEM.

REFERENCES

Here's a list of books that I have read and I would recommend if you want to learn more about paleontology. Some helpful websites are listed below, and also some terrific dinosaur documentaries.

BOOKS
The Amazing Dinosaur Quiz Book, DK
The Complete Idiot's Guide to Dinosaurs, Alpha Books
Deep Alberta, The University of Alberta Press
Dinosaur Digs, Discovery Communications Inc.
Dinosaurs, Discover Prehistoric Life, Miles Kelly Publishing
First Dinosaur Encyclopedia, DK
How to be a Dinosaur Hunter, Lonely Planet
The Illustrated Encyclopedia of Dinosaurs and Prehistoric Creatures, Oceana Books
Introducing Paleontology, A Guide to Ancient Life, Dunedin
Prehistoric Life, DK
The Princeton Field Guide to Dinosaurs, Princeton University Press
Pocket Genius: Dinosaurs, DK
The Usborne World Atlas, Usborne
The Ultimate Dinopedia, National Geographic Kids
Visual Encyclopedia of Dinosaurs, DK

WEBSITES
http://news.discovery.com/animals/dinosaurs
http://www.kidsdinos.com/
http://dinohuntcanada.history.ca/#!/
http://discoverykids.com/category/dinosaurs/
http://kids.nationalgeographic.com/explore/nature/dinosaurs/
http://www.sheppardsoftware.com/scienceforkids/dinosaurs/index.htm

DOCUMENTARIES
Walking with Dinosaurs, BBC
Walking with Monsters, BBC

MUSEUMS
Here are some museums that I've been to and strongly recommend. My favorites are in England.

- Redpath Museum, McGill University, Montreal, Quebec
- Canadian Museum of Nature, Ottawa, Ontario
- Royal Tyrell Museum, Drumheller, Alberta
- American Museum of Natural History, New York, New York
- Field Museum of Natural History, Chicago, Illinois
- Natural History Museum of Los Angeles County, Los Angeles, California
- Natural History Museum, London, England
- Oxford University Museum of Natural History, Oxford, England

GLOSSARY

amphibians: creatures that can live both in water and on land.

archosaurs: "ruling reptiles" were the direct ancestors of the dinosaurs and also the common ancestor of birds and crocodiles.

ceratopsians: plant-eating dinosaurs in the ornithischian order; they walked on four legs and were notable (with some exceptions) for their enormous heads with horns and frills.

cursorial: a creature that is described as cursorial has a body shape that is adapted to running very quickly.

evolution: the process by which species change across many generations.

graviportal: a creature that is described as graviportal has a body shape that is adapted to moving slowly over land, supporting a high body weight.

mass extinction: the dying off of a large number of species, possibly due to an environmental change or a catastrophic event.

ornithiscian: ornithiscian means "bird-hipped"; these dinosaurs have a bird-like configuration of their hip bones, even though they are not closely related to birds.

paleontologists: scientists who study the geologic past through the study of fossils.

Pangaea: a single land mass that later divided and drifted apart to create all the continents on Earth today.

reptiles: cold-blooded vertebrates that lay eggs; marine reptiles: reptiles that can live in the ocean.

saurischian: saurischian means "lizard-hipped"; these dinosaurs have a lizard-like configuration of their hip bones.

sauropods: plant-eating dinosaurs in the saurischian order that walked on four legs; they typically grew to enormous sizes.

terrestrial vascular plants: land plants that have structures to conduct water and minerals.

theropods: meat-eating dinosaurs in the saurischian order that walked on two legs; birds are theropods.

vertebrates: animals distinguished by the possession of a backbone or spinal column, including mammals, birds, reptiles, amphibians, and fishes.

ACKNOWLEDGMENTS

I'd like to thank the many people who helped me with this project:

- Christine Cade, for her excellent paleontology classes and her work as a graphic designer;

- Hans Larsson, paleontologist, for his support, his help with fact-checking, and his invitation to the Canadian Paleontology Conference at McGill University;

- Marguerite-Bourgeoys School Board, for allowing me to take classes with Christine;

- my parents, for their help with my research;

- Les Éditions MultiMondes, for agreeing to publish my book;

- Greystone Books, for translating and publishing my book in English.

PHOTO CREDITS

The editor would like to thank the following people and organizations for their permission to reproduce the following photos:

(LEGEND – b: bottom; c: centre; r: right; l: left; t: top)

6 **iStock:** julos (c).

8 **iStock:** julos (c). **Photo of Elliott Seah:** Isabelle Champagne (cr).

9 **Photo of Hans Larsson, Christine Cade, and Elliott Seah:** Mario Cournoyer (cr).

10 **Vectorportal:** Robb Kottmyer (tl). **Dollar Photo Club:** fergregory (ct). **iStock:** Susan Montgomery (bl). **Wikipedia:** Paolo Sacch1 (cb).

11 **BBC News:** Junchang Lu (ct). **National Geographic:** Chuang Zhao (cr). **iStock:** julos (br).

12 **Colorado Plateau Geosystems, Inc.:** Ron Blakey (cl). **iStock:** julos (br). **karencarr.com:** Karen Carr (bl).

13 **Science Photo Library:** Stephen J. Krasemann (tl). **Dollar Photo Club:** Catmando (b).

14 **Shutterstock:** Kostyantyn Ivanyshen (t). **PhyloPic:** Charles Doolittle Walcott (vectorized by T Michael Keesey) (bl). **PhyloPic:** Dmitry Bogdanov (vectorized by T. Michael Keesey) (br).

15 **Colorado Plateau Geosystems, Inc.:** Ron Blakey (cl). **PhyloPic:** Michael P. Taylor (bl). **PhyloPic:** Scott Hartman (bl) **PhyloPic:** Gareth Monger (br). **PhyloPic:** Lukasiniho (br).

16 **iStock:** Mark Kostich (cl). **Alamy:** Craig Larcom (c). **Science Photo Library:** Natural History Museum. London (cr). **Science Photo Library:** Natural History Museum. London (b).

17 **iStock:** Julos (tr). **Thinkstock:** Darling Kindersley (bl). **Thinkstock:** Darling Kindersley (br).

18 **Thinkstock:** Elenarts (tr). **iStock:** CoreyFord (bl). **iStock:** jules (br).

19 **Shutterstock:** Jaroslav Moravcik (tr). **Thinkstock:** CoreyFord (br).

20 **Science Photo Library:** Julius T Csotonyi (tr). **Dollar Photo Club:** Katja Xenikis (br).

21 **Shutterstock:** Phil Holmes (cr). **Science Photo Library:** Leonelle Calvetti (b).

24 **Science Photo Library:** Gary Hincks (tl). **Dollar Photo Club:** fergregory (tr). **Science Photo Library:** Friedrich Saurer (br).

25 **Shutterstock:** Michael Rosskothen (cl). **iStock:** leonello (bl).

26 **Science Photo Library:** Jose Antonio Peiias (tr,b).

27 **Science Photo Library:** Friedrich Saurer (tr). **iStock:** breckeni (br).

30 **Science Photo Library:** Leonello Calvetti (tr). **Shutterstock:** Linda Bucklin (c).

31 **Science Photo Library:** Leonello Calvetti (tr). **iStock:** mariephoto28 (br).

32 **Science Photo Library:** Jose Antonio Peiias (tr, br).

33 **Shutterstock:** Catmando (tr). **Science Photo Library:** Natural History Museum. London (bl,br).

36 **Shutterstock:** dimair (tr). **Shutterstock:** Ozja (br).

37 **iStock:** leoneiie (tr, cl). **iStock:** JaysonPhotography (bl).

38 **Shutterstock:** Evgeniy Mahnyov (tr). **Science Photo library:** Jose Antonio Peiias (bl).

39 **Science Photo Library:** Jose Antonio Peiias (tr, bl). **Shutterstock:** Herschel Hoffmeyer (br).

40 **Thinkstock:** James Thew (b).

41 **Thinkstock:** James Thew (b).

42 **Dollar Photo Club:** birdiegal (tr). **Shutterstock:** Ozja (bl).

43 **Shutterstock:** njaj (c). **Thinkstock:** CoreyFord (bl).

44 **Shutterstock:** Rich Keele (t). **Thinkstock:** SiriStafford (bl).

45 **Thinkstock:** Garsya (tr). **Shutterstock:** Darkkong (cl). **iStock:** jules (bl).

Images throughout the book:
(Planet earth) **Thinkstock:** artsstock.
(Black and white images, p.44-45) **Thinkstock:** Kapreski.